THE SUN INSIDE CLOSED EYES

BY
STEPHEN L. AVARD, JR., J.D.

ISBN: 0-615-54379-0
ISBN-13: 978-0-615-54379-6
LCCN: 2011917444
Avard Enterprises LLC, Kingwood, TX

This book is dedicated to past,

present, and future believers.

"...and his face was like the sun shining in full strength."

The Revelation to John 1: 16.

TABLE OF CONTENTS

PART ONE:

PART TWO:

PART THREE:

PART ONE

POWER

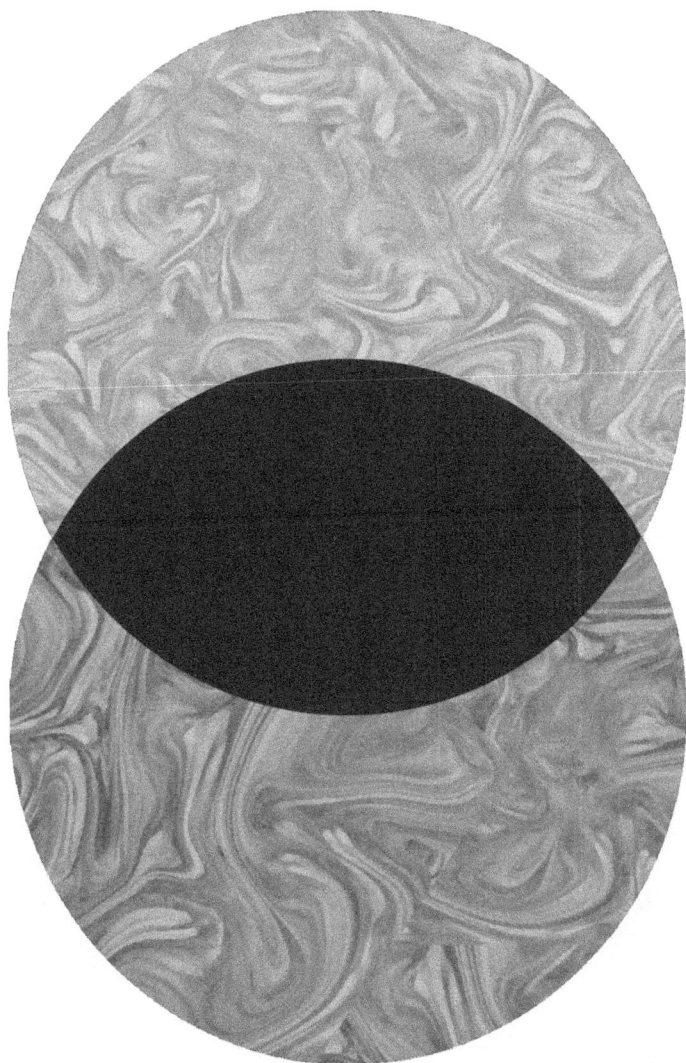

CHAPTER 1

"Hence I remind you to rekindle the gift of God that is within you through the laying on of my hands; for God did not give us a spirit of timidity but a spirit of power and love and self-control."

The Second Letter of Paul
to Timothy 1: 6 and 7

Greetings, Beloved, from beyond space and time. The gift has been given to you from outside of space and time. Grace is yours. Your spirit is waiting. God is power, His Son is love, and The Holy Spirit gives you self-control. Amen.

Close your eyes.

What do you see? Is there any light within the darkness?

Are you unhappy? What happened to your childhood dreams? Where are your dreams today?

Does Las Vegas make you happy? Does your stuffed home and over-packed garage make you content? Do images on the internet of things you want give you happiness? Do you love your car? Your clothes? Your jewelry? Do you fantasize about sexual immorality? Do you lust after what you do not, or cannot, have?

Have you felt one moment of pure joy? Let's face it. You are lost. You are lost in your sin. Sin is more than an old-fashioned word. Sin is an ancient word. What is your sin of the day? You want a better life. You want a good life. You want to be happy. Perhaps, after all, it is your wants that are blocking your happiness. Do you complain of want? Have you learned, in whatever state you are in, to be content? Do you know the secret of facing plenty and hunger, abundance and want? (See *Philippians 4: 11–13*)

I mowed the yard for the first time after my wife and I moved into our first home years ago. The biggest tree in the backyard was what we call, in South Texas, a cedar or mountain cedar. It is actually an Ashe Juniper. The tree is an ugly water-hog.

A large, blooming yucca was also in the backyard. It was taller than me. It had beautiful white flowers. It had needle-like leaves to protect the flowers. The yucca had been there a long time, probably decades. This was the yucca's turf. The DeZavala Ranch was long gone, but the yucca survived suburban encroachments.

I pushed the lawnmower in row after row, not far from the yucca and close to the newly-built house. I came upon a thin shoot or sprout sticking out of the ground. It was not as tall as my knee. It was thinner than a pencil. It had one tiny leaf on it.

Chapter 1

"Is this a weed?" I asked myself as I stopped the lawnmower.

Close your eyes again. What do you see? Darkness? Light? What do the insides of your eyelids look like? Are these your two eyes or your mind's eye? Are you looking at yourself when your eyes are closed? Do you have power? Love? Self-control? How can you get power, love, and self-control? Learn to see the sun shining inside your closed eyes. Let go. You will be found.

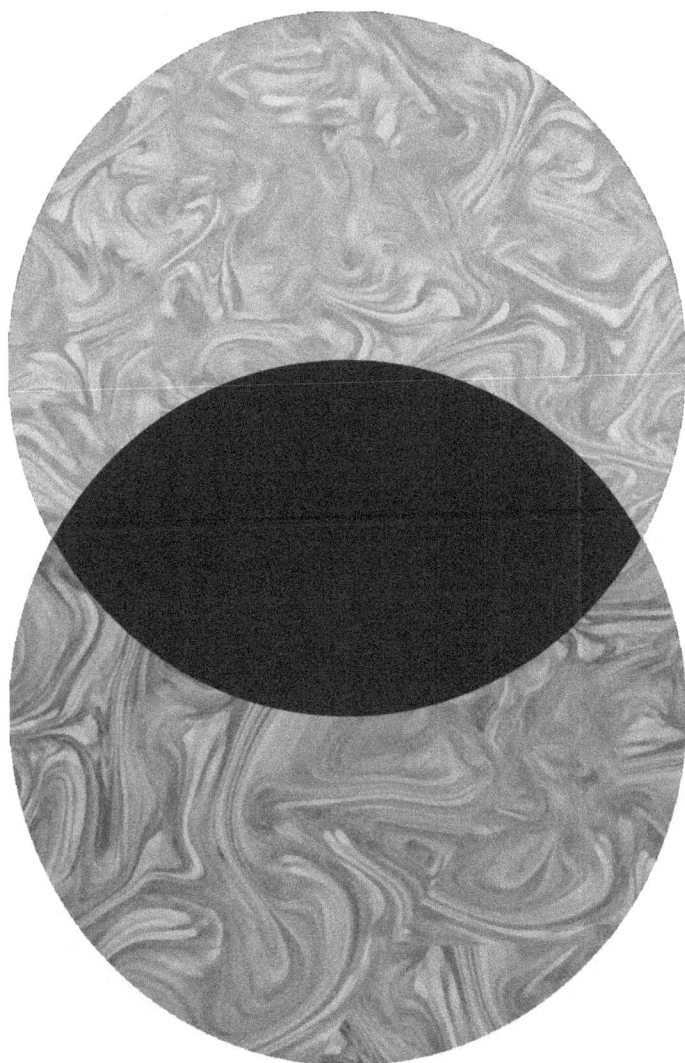

CHAPTER 2

Mysticism is not dead, but it is lost. Mysticism is not magic or sorcery. Mysticism is a spiritual discipline aiming at direct union or communion with ultimate reality or God through deep meditation or contemplation. You must transform your mind to rediscover spiritual discipline.

The Star of Bethlehem is real. You can see that Star when your eyes are closed. The stars are brighter than our world. The Star of Bethlehem is brighter than the stars.

Dedicate twenty minutes per day to the following meditation and you will begin to see the sun inside closed eyes. Say the words in your mind in the left/Breathe In column then say the words in your mind in the right/Breathe Out column as you breathe. The first group would go, "Breathe In, Breathe Out; Breathe In, Breathe Out; Breathe In, Breathe Out." Continue to the end with this pattern of breathing and word focus.

MEDITATION

BREATHE IN	BREATHE OUT
Breathe In	Breathe Out
Breathe In	Breathe Out
Breathe In	Breathe Out
God loves me	I love God
God loves me	I love God
God loves me	I love God
I am present, open,	and awake
I am present, open,	and awake
I am present, open,	and awake
Here I am,	Lord
Here I am,	Lord
Here I am,	Lord
Be still	and know that I am the Lord
Be still	and know that I am the Lord
Be still	and know that I am the Lord
Be still	and know
Be still	and know
Be still	and know

BREATHE IN	BREATHE OUT
Be	still
Be	still
Be	still
Be	
Be	
Be	
Adonai	Sovereignty and My Lord
Adonai	Sovereignty and My Lord
Adonai	Sovereignty and My Lord
El Shaddai	Foundation
El Shaddai	Foundation
El Shaddai	Foundation
Elohim	Judgment
Elohim	Judgment
Elohim	Judgment
Yahweh	Wisdom and Understanding
Yahweh	Wisdom and Understanding
Yahweh	Wisdom and Understanding

The Sun Inside Closed Eyes

BREATHE IN	BREATHE OUT
Ehyeh	Crown of Humility
Ehyeh	Crown of Humility
Ehyeh	Crown of Humility
Jesus	God with us
Jesus	God with us
Jesus	God with us
Holy Spirit	In-dwelling
Holy Spirit	In-dwelling
Holy Spirit	In-dwelling
Father, Son,	and Holy Ghost
Father, Son,	and Holy Ghost
Father, Son,	and Holy Ghost
Holy	Trinity
Holy	Trinity
Holy	Trinity
Power, Love, and	Self-Control
Power, Love, and	Self-Control
Power, Love, and	Self-Control

BREATHE IN	BREATHE OUT
I can do all things in Him	who strengthens me
I can do all things in Him	who strengthens me
I can do all things in Him	who strengthens me
God loves me	I love God
God loves me	I love God
God loves me	I love God
Breathe In	Breathe Out
Breathe In	Breathe Out
Breathe In	Breathe Out.

Something (Instinct? Indecision? Curiosity? The Holy Spirit?) told me I should not cut down the shoot in the backyard. I did not let my lawnmower move.

"I have never seen a weed that looked like that," I thought. "I'm gonna let it grow for a while and see what it turns into." I did not mow it down. I mowed around that little sprout.

Twenty minutes of the above meditation per day can relax your body, calm your mind, and bring you into internal union with your soul. Look within to meet God. Close your eyes and prepare yourself. You will be amazed at what you find.

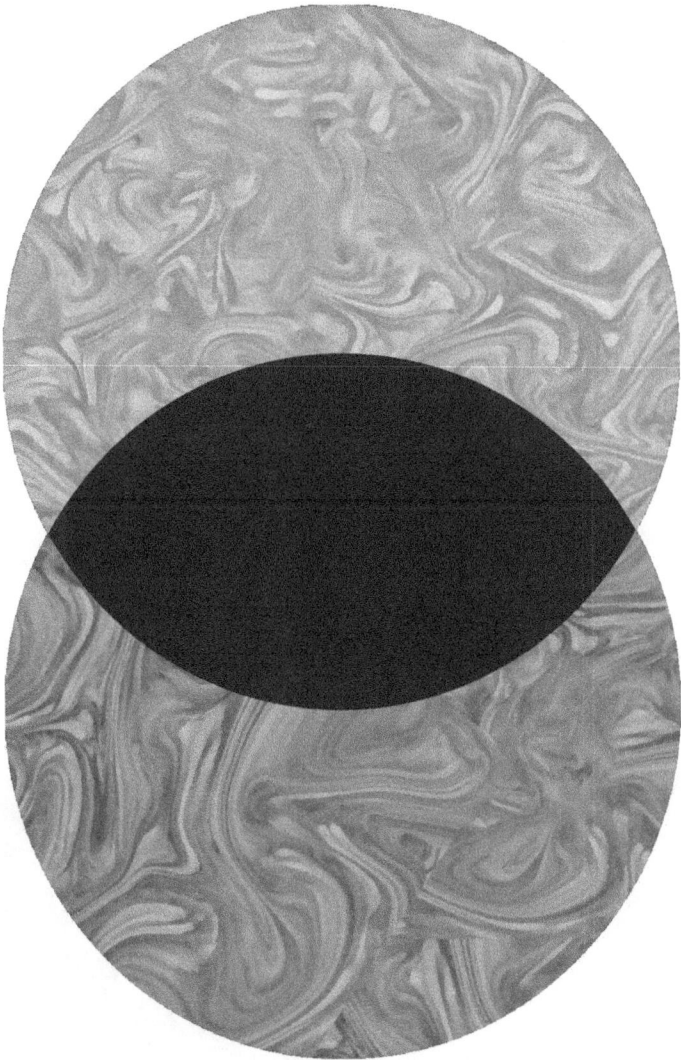

CHAPTER 3

People have objections. Of course they do. We live in the information age. It is also the age of materialism, the age of science, and the age of quantification. Isn't this additionally the age of connectivity?

Some people believe mysticism is for fools, children, and psychics. How can mysticism be important to us in the age of discovery? Why is mysticism relevant, or even probative, in a time of space travel, interstellar telescopes, galactic probes, atom-splitting, DNA analysis and manipulation, and humanity's domination over all things earthly and material?

We must begin with your soul. Soul is defined as the animating and vital principle in man, credited with the faculties of thought, action and emotion, and often conceived as an immaterial entity. That is a broad definition, isn't it? Maybe a better definition of soul includes words to the effect that we know what it is, but we can't put a finger on it.

If someone does not believe in the concept of a soul, this book is not for them. If somebody needs a microscope or a telescope to examine important subjects, this book is not for them.

However, if you believe in your soul, then you are knocking on the right door. *The Sun Inside Closed Eyes* is an introduction to your one true self; your eternal self, for better or for worse.

But let's not get ahead of ourselves, because we must overcome possible objections before we take our first steps on the inward path.

Science, in the twentieth and twenty-first centuries, is impressive. One could venture to state that more has been discovered, learned, documented, recorded, and quantified in the past hundred years than in all of the previous centuries combined. Man has traveled to the moon and back, split the atom, detonated nuclear bombs, mapped the human genome, invented vaccines, created smart phones and microscopic computers, learned how to fly, and investigated molecular universes.

You can videotape, record, photograph, and digitize your favorite subject. You can, with enough money, become a space tourist. You are connected to people on the other side of the world through email, instant communication, and satellites.

But for all of its accomplishments, Science has failed on the big subjects:

1. Who are we and where did we come from?

2. Where are we going?

3. What is the meaning of human life?

4. How do we cure cancer?

5. How do we end war?

6. Why do we die?

7. How can we overcome death?

8. Where does our soul go when we die?

9. Where is heaven? Is it in another galaxy or in another dimension?

10. How do we find love?

About 2,000 years ago Jesus Christ overcame the objections of the age of discovery and material observation. Luke 17: 20–21 states, "And when he was demanded of the Pharisees, when the kingdom of God should come, he answered them and said, 'The kingdom of God cometh not with observation: Neither shall they say, Lo here! Or, lo there! For, behold, the kingdom of God is within you.'"

Is the kingdom of God within you? Or are you waiting to see? Are you waiting to see and to say, "Here it is!" or "There it is!"? Is your telescope in your hand? Do you grip your microscope or video-recorder? Where are you looking? Put your scientific tools away and take a hold of the most powerful tool of humanity: your spiritual life within. Close your eyes to see.

When they visited our backyard, our friends and neighbors would comment on the curved shoot and say, "What is that little thing? It looks so funny. You should cut it down."

I would smile and say, "That's my little experiment. I am going to let it grow and see what happens." They looked at me like I was crazy.

"I don't know what it is, but I'm willing to give it a fightin' chance," I told them.

The metaphysical is not removed from the physical. They are interconnected. The scientist and the preacher are not as different as you may think. But let's get back to your soul.

Where inside of you is your soul located? There have been many guesses throughout the ages: the soul is located in your heart, the soul is located in your mind, the soul is your breath. The soul is biochemical or cellular. The soul is in the strength of your muscles. What do you think? Where is your soul to be pinpointed?

Chapter 3

The Holy Bible says "For the life of the flesh is in the blood..." and "For the life of every creature is the blood of it..." (See *Leviticus 17: 11 and 14*). I don't know what that means exactly or scientifically, but I believe it.

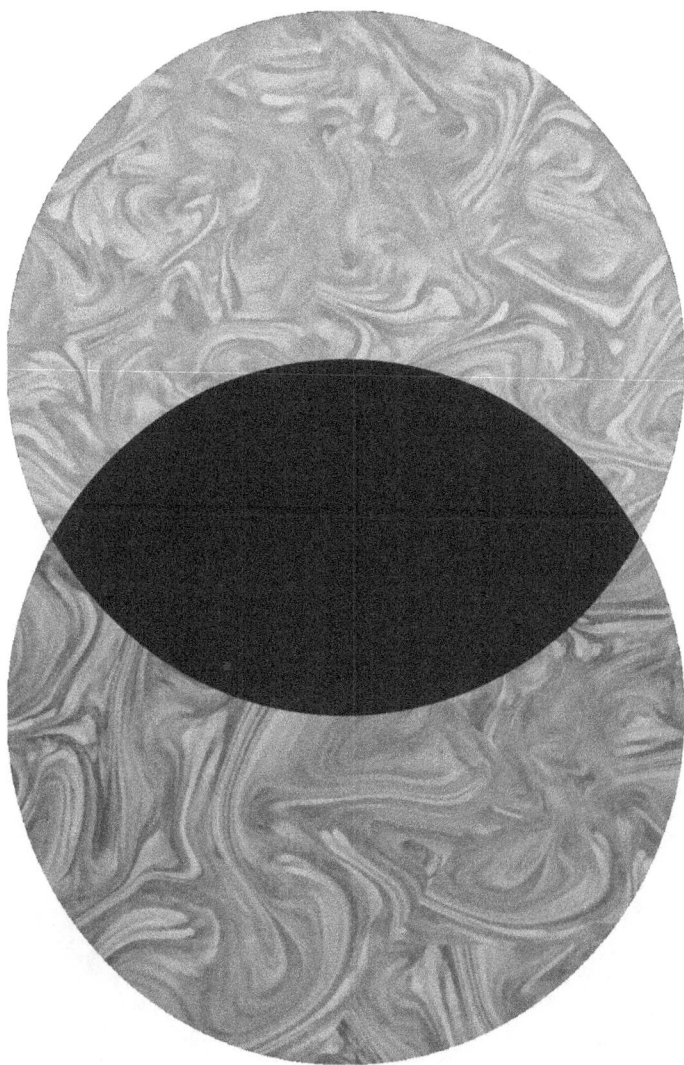

CHAPTER 4

"Rekindle the gift of God that is within you." What does that mean? The verb "rekindle" is important. According to *The American Heritage Dictionary*, "rekindle" means to kindle anew (as of a fire), to revive, to arouse or cause to be aroused again, to relight (a fire), and to renew. So, we are told to relight, or renew, or revive the gift within ourselves, like a fire.

What is this fire within?

What is this gift within?

Where is the match? Where is the lighter?

There is, without a doubt, a gift of God that is within you. Think about that phrase, "the gift of God." Free your mind, because it is conditioned improperly: when you read the word "gift," you imagine or visualize a box that is gift wrapped and contains a material item that you treasure. How foolish are we in the twenty-first century!

A gift is something that is bestowed voluntarily and without compensation. It is a talent, endowment, aptitude, or bent.

We say, "She is a gifted artist." We say, "That boy is a gifted athlete." It is a figure of speech that is a substitute for "talented." But it may be that "the gift of God that is within you" refers only to your spirit and not to your talents. Talents are addressed elsewhere in The Holy Scriptures.

In the context of the entire passage, the writer is teaching about some characteristics of the human spirit; not timidity, but, power and love and self-control. Saint Paul is describing our souls. He is emphasizing that they are bestowed voluntarily and without compensation. You did not buy your soul. You did not barter for your soul. God bestowed your soul upon you voluntarily. It is a gift to you, from Him.

This gift is not a material thing or, in the terminology of economics, a durable good. It is not something to be consumed. It is a spiritual gift to be *rekindled*. The verb is up to you. We must relight the gift inside of us. It is already there; it was lit once; it is waiting to be relit by you. You do not have to start a fire within. You simply have to restart it. Get it going again. Fill the darkness with your light. Reignite. There are always embers of "soul fire" to revive within us.

One thing about my thin shoot is that I did not plant it. It was there when we moved in. It looked so frail behind a large mountain cedar and a menacing yucca. However, I did consciously choose not to mow it down, and to give it time to grow to see what it would become.

Chapter 4

It was bowed outward, and the way it came out of the ground at an odd angle looked funny. It had been reaching out desperately for the sunshine since the day it first came out of the ground. That skinny reed of a plant was fighting to get out from the shadows of the yucca and the cedar tree from its birth. It wanted the sun. It curved itself. It distorted itself. It reached for its life and its existence. The cedar and the yucca cast wide and ominous shadows across the yard. But our sad sprout stretched for the sunlight with every inch of its being.

Let's return to Luke. Luke 17: 20–21 states, "And when he was demanded of the Pharisees, when the kingdom of God should come, he answered them and said, 'The kingdom of God cometh not with observation: Neither shall they say, Lo here! Or, lo there! For, behold, the kingdom of God is within you.'"

Could it be that "the gift of God that is within you" is the "kingdom of God"? What does that mean to you? Can we translate this to mean "your soul is the kingdom of God"? As Romans 12:11 says, "…be aglow with the Spirit…"

What is this kingdom? This kingdom is the eternal spiritual sovereignty of God. This is not an earthly or political or geographic kingdom. This is the Living God's eternal *spiritual* universe, within you and within me. If God created a spiritual survey map with markers, pins, and stakes, you are included within the metes and bounds. You have the power. "The kingdom of God is within you."

x

PART TWO

LOVE

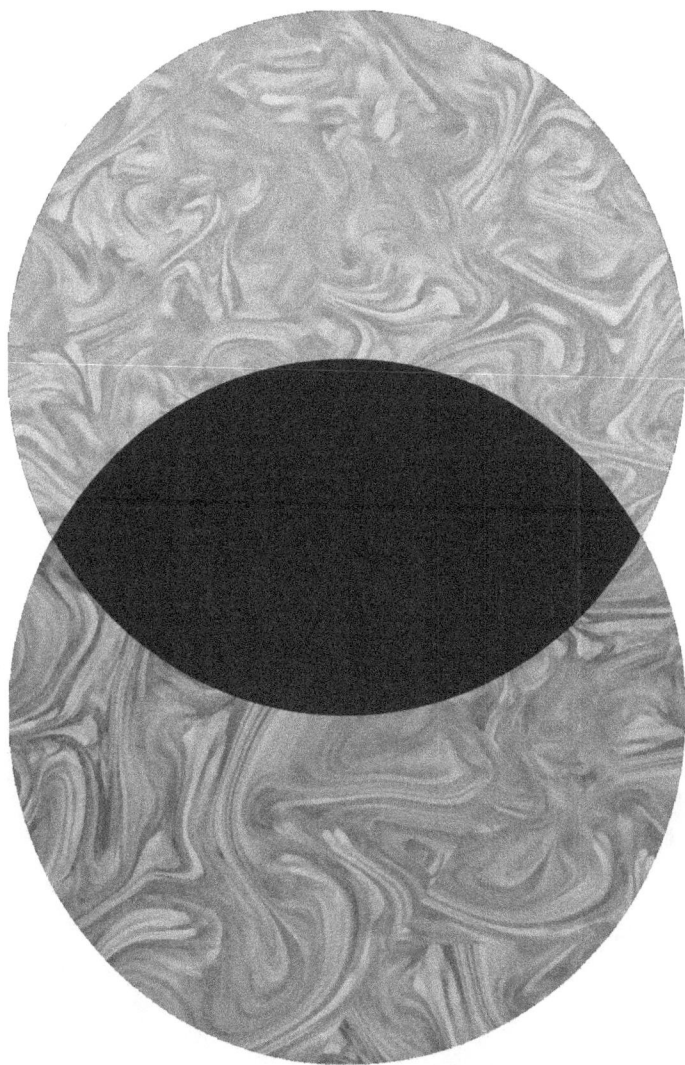

CHAPTER 5

"Hence I remind you to rekindle the gift of God that is within you through the laying on of my hands; for God did not give us a spirit of timidity but a spirit of power and love and self-control."

The Second Letter of Paul
to Timothy 1: 6 and 7

The thing about love is not that it is easy, but that it is hard. The door is narrow, the path is straight, and the way is difficult. This world is not on your side.

Love is important for many reasons, but it is an especially important fruit of the Christian meditation tradition. Meditation is not meant to isolate us or to withdraw us from the world into a hermit-like existence of solitude. Quite the contrary: Christian meditation will lead us to a greater ability and willingness to love. The contemplative path can help us to love God, to love ourselves, and to love others.

I knew a man once; he hired me for a construction job when I was young. He had two sons in elementary school. The oldest son was adopted.

The father was at the barbershop one morning. The barber asked him how his sons were doing, and he said, "Fine."

The barber said, "Now, which one of them is adopted?"

The father said, "I don't know. I forget."

Who do you love? Do you only love those people who love you? Do you love strangers? Do you love the poor? Do you love the weak? The widow? The orphan? The immigrant?

Do you love your neighbor? The mean old lady next door? The neighbor who is dealing drugs through her teenagers. Do you love the snobs on your street who won't talk to you because they think they are better than you? Do you love the family that is ethnically different than you?

Take it to the next level. Do you love your enemy? Do you love your worst enemy? Do you love all of your enemies?

The cedar in our backyard grew aggressively. It invaded space with its greed for water. Its leaves were ugly and abrasive to the touch. The bark was straggly and unkempt.

The yucca poked and jabbed me in the arms and chest. I was pricked by the yucca's needles so many times that I learned to keep my distance. I would not touch it for a number of years. Finally, its overgrowth of dead, long leaves demanded my attention. I carefully pulled away the dead leaves with their angry needles.

I received scratches and stabs as I gave the yucca much-needed attention. I made slow progress with patience and persistence. The yucca started to look youthful and slender again after its fat and slumping years. It stood up because it had less weight bringing it down. The number of flowers and the size of the flower-canopy doubled the next year. I hauled away the dead leaves, needles and all. The yucca became my friend.

Do you love the one who betrayed you? Your former friend? Your past business partner? Your first spouse? The old boss who fired you? The people who interviewed you, but did not hire you? The woman who got the promotion that you had coming?

Yes, the thing about love is not that it is easy, but that it is hard. Listen to Mark, in Chapter 12, Verses 28–34:

"And one of the scribes came up and heard them disputing with one another, and seeing that he answered them well, asked him, 'Which commandment is the first of all?' Jesus answered, 'The first is, 'Hear, O Israel: The Lord our God, the Lord is one; and you shall love the Lord your God with all your heart, and with all your soul, and with all your mind, and with all your strength.' The second is this, 'You shall love your neighbor as yourself.' There is no other commandment greater than these.' And the scribe said to him, 'You are right, Teacher; you have truly said that he is one, and there is no other but he; and to love him with all the heart, and with all the understanding, and with all the strength, and to love one's neighbor as oneself, is much more than all whole burnt offerings and sacrifices.' And when Jesus saw that he answered wisely, he said to him, 'You are not far from the kingdom of God.' And after that no one dared to ask him any question."

Do you love your neighbor as yourself? Do you love all of your neighbors as yourself? Or do you love them less than you love yourself? Or do you not love them at all? Or do you tolerate them? Or do you hate them? Admit to yourself that you have some neighbors that you cannot stand.

Maybe it is too much to ask right now for you to love your neighbor as yourself. Maybe we need to take a step back. Maybe you need to learn to love yourself before you can do any other loving. What, after all, is so special about you?

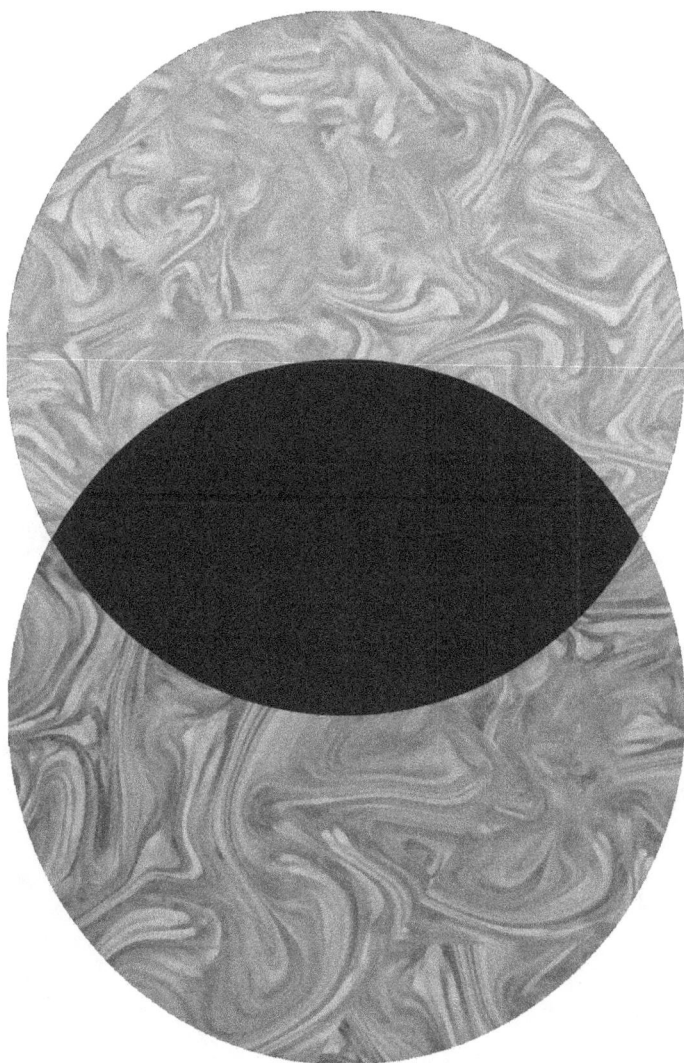

CHAPTER 6

The most important thing about you is that you have the ability to love. God did not give you a spirit of timidity, but a spirit of love.

Many people think and talk about their loved ones on their death beds. In summarizing our lives, the tally at the end is not about what you bought, what you had, and who you defeated. The only questions that matter are: Did you love God with all of your being? Did you love your neighbor as yourself? How much did you love? How many did you love? Did you forgive your enemy and love him?

When you meet your Maker, do you believe that your Maker will ask, "How much money did you accumulate? Did you drive the most expensive car? Was your house the biggest? Did you take the most fabulous vacations? Does your watch have the most diamonds?"

It is more likely that your Maker will ask, "How did you respond to the person who hurt you the most in the world? What did you do for the least among you? Did you help the sick? Did you feed the poor? Did you give the stranger your coat? Did you love your enemies? Did you love your neigh-bors? Did you love me with all of your heart, mind, soul, and strength? Did you love me at all?"

One day years ago, I realized that my shoot was a live oak sapling. I watched it more often when I realized what it was and that it was not a weed. I started to care about it. The situation had transformed from my experiment to my stewardship. I cared. I wanted that sprout of a tree to live and grow. I wanted the shoot to become a tree.

This is not easy stuff. The sun inside closed eyes must first be seen. Then it must be shared. If you can enter the kingdom of God (which, of course you know by now is found within you), then you can share it with your neighbor and a stranger.

The kingdom of God does not have forts, castles, borders, or fences. The kingdom of God knows no nationalities or ethnic groups. The kingdom of God does not have gates. The kingdom of God is not confined to the third planet from the sun in this solar system. The kingdom of God is not confined to The Milky Way Galaxy or the galaxy next door. The kingdom of God is not confined to heaven or to heaven-to-come-on-earth.

The kingdom of God is within you. The kingdom of God is inside of dimensions that human beings have yet to discover or comprehend. The gift of God is your spirit, not of timidity, but of power, love, and self-control.

There are many avenues to the kingdom of God. They include, but are not limited to, reading scripture and inspired books, prayer, meditation and contemplation, worship, fellowship, gifts, service, and love.

Prayer and meditation should be contrasted. Prayer is how you communicate with God. It is you "talking" to God. You praise him, confess to him, give thanks to him, and make your petitions and supplications to him. You are executing the verbs in prayer. You are the actor and the speaker.

Meditation, in contrast, is a way for you to invite God to communicate with you. It is you listening, but it is not passive listening. You must be an active listener. Go back and review Chapter 2 about meditation. The focus is not on you and your prayers, pains, hopes, and wishes. The focus is on creating and contemplating, within yourself, an invitation for God to come closer. Close your eyes to see the sun. You must "leave" yourself to be in meditative communion with the ultimate reality, God.

Don't you want to feel the mystery? Don't you want to experience the totality, infinite and minuscule, that is eternity and divinity? You invite the kingdom of God to come closer to your heart and soul when you meditate on God and

God's love for you. This is not about intellectual knowledge of God but, rather, it is about experiencing God with your eyes closed. If you can learn to do this, your love for yourself will blossom through hard work. You will begin to see clearly. With your eyes closed, in daily meditation, God's kingdom will approach. You will get the spark.

The spark is to love: to love God; to love your neighbor; to love your neighbor as yourself. If you can control yourself, you can learn to listen to the Alpha and the Omega. You can learn to love the Beginning and the End by listening and by looking for the light when your eyes are closed. The Lord says to Isaiah, "...and shut their eyes; lest they see with their eyes..." (See *Isaiah 6: 10*)

It is simply amazing what happens when you stop focusing on yourself and concentrate on The Evermore. Your meditation, after months and years, can move you from contemplation of Divine Love to active loving of your neighbors and enemies. You must see, by now, that it is all the same. The commandments to love God and to love your neighbor as yourself become blurred and blended. They are not distinct, but inseparable. When you love God, you love your neighbor. When you love your neighbor, you love God.

The mystery is revealed. The cloud of unknowing lifts. You have fed your shoot with water, sunshine, and love. You invited love in. Love came. Now you have to share it. You want to share it. You want to love because you are loved. This is the gift of God. You cannot take credit for it. In some ways, this is not about you. "...[F]or God is at work in you, both to will and to work for his good pleasure." (See *Philippians 2:13*) This is grace. You have been gifted grace from beyond space and time. You are outside of space and time. Although you cannot see it, you can feel the face of God, shining like the sun in full strength. It is the blanketing warmth of eternity. You want to pass it on. You are rekindling the gift of God that is within you.

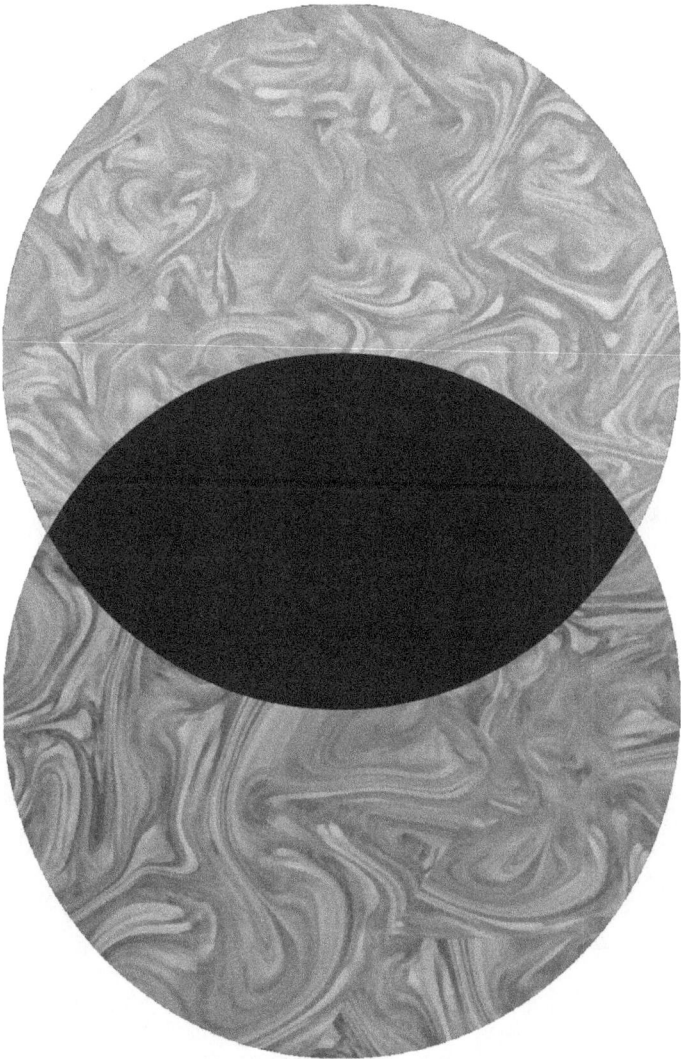

CHAPTER 7

"...[T]hrough the laying on of my hands..." Touch is important to love. The American Medical Association has reported that babies who are held and touched more, grow faster than babies who are not. Isn't that incredible? It is scientific proof of the power of love. Touch more and love more; grow faster.

What is touch? Touch (the verb), per *The American Heritage Dictionary*, means "...to cause or permit a part of the body, esp. the hand or fingers, to come in contact with so as to feel." So, touching is associated with feeling. Love is not an abstraction. Love involves touching and feeling. It is a matter of the heart. The heart is master of feelings. Science also indicates that there is a connection between emotion and contact. Physical touch and emotional touch work together for the sake of love.

How do we define love? It is difficult to beat Chapter 13 of Paul's First Letter to The Corinthians:

"If I speak in the tongues of men and of angels, but have not love, I am a noisy gong or a clanging cymbal. And if I have prophetic powers, and understand all mysteries and all knowledge, and if I have all faith, so as to remove mountains, but have not love, I am nothing. If I give away all that I have, and if I deliver my body to be burned, but have not love, I gain nothing.

Love is patient and kind; love is not jealous or boastful; it is not arrogant or rude. Love does not insist on its own way; it is not irritable or resentful; it does not rejoice at wrong, but rejoices in right. Love bears all things, believes all things, hopes all things, endures all things.

Love never ends; as for prophecies, they will pass away; as for tongues, they will cease; as for knowledge, it will pass away. For our knowledge is imperfect and our prophecy is imperfect; but when the perfect comes, the imperfect will pass away. When I was a child, I spoke like a child, I thought like a child, I reasoned like a child; when I became a man, I gave up childish ways. For now we see in a mirror dimly, but then face to face. Now I know in part; then I shall understand fully, even as I have been fully understood. So faith, hope, love abide, these three; but the greatest of these is love."

This is what love is. Love is not a photograph, video, or image on the internet or smart phone. Love is not ruled by a telecom company or a corporation's satellite. Love is not an affair with a partner outside of your marriage. Love is not egomania, self-centeredness, or narcissism.

Hear it again: "Love is patient and kind; love is not jealous or boastful; it is not arrogant or rude. Love does not insist on its own way; it is not irritable or resentful; it does not rejoice at wrong, but rejoices in right. Love bears all things, believes all things, hopes all things, endures all things."

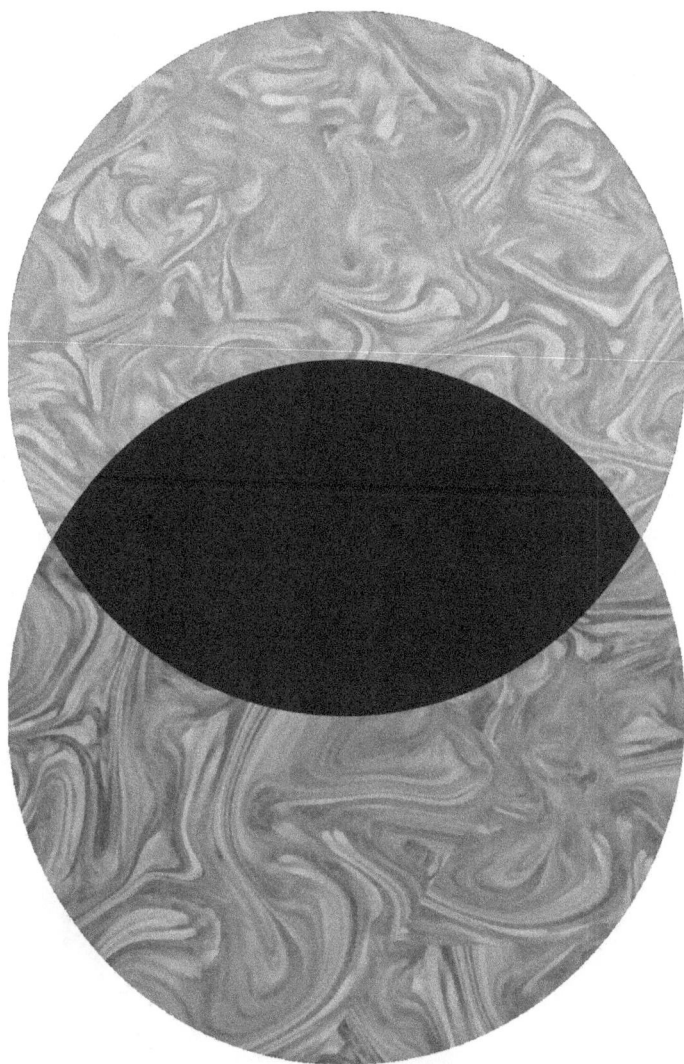

CHAPTER 8

"Let brotherly love continue. Do not neglect to show hospitality to strangers, for thereby some have entertained angels unawares."

Hebrews 13: 1 and 2

It is easy to love those we know, those we already love, and those whose love we seek. It is not easy to love "the different." How hard is it to show hospitality to strangers? The people at the traffic signal with their hands out? The disturbed man who talks to himself on the downtown street and approaches you for change? Strangers you see when you travel? When you are out of your hospitality zone?

I cannot tell you how many times I have looked away when a hand approached my window while I sat in my car at a traffic light. My first thoughts are "How do I know this person will use this money for food or something good? Why should I give my money so he can go buy booze or drugs?"

"Entertained angels unawares." That is a powerful thought. Angels cross our paths and we are "unawares." We don't know it. We don't know they are angels. We don't know angels are crossing our paths. God sent angels where we see strangers. God plays with us, it is true. But divine play is for our own good. We were blind but now we see. The next time a hand approaches you, remember that you might entertain an angel unawares.

Strangers in The Holy Bible seem to be, in modern constitutional words, a protected class. Widows and orphans are other protected classes in The Testaments. How many references to lost sheep are there in The Holy Words? Take care of widows and orphans when they cross your path. The Lord is teaching us that there are certain people (strangers, aliens, widows, lost sheep, and orphans) who can use our love and kindness. Be on the lookout for these protected classes. Remember, but for the Grace of God, there goes you. Perhaps one day you will be a widow or a stranger or a lost sheep. Entertain angels unaware.

PART THREE

SELF-CONTROL

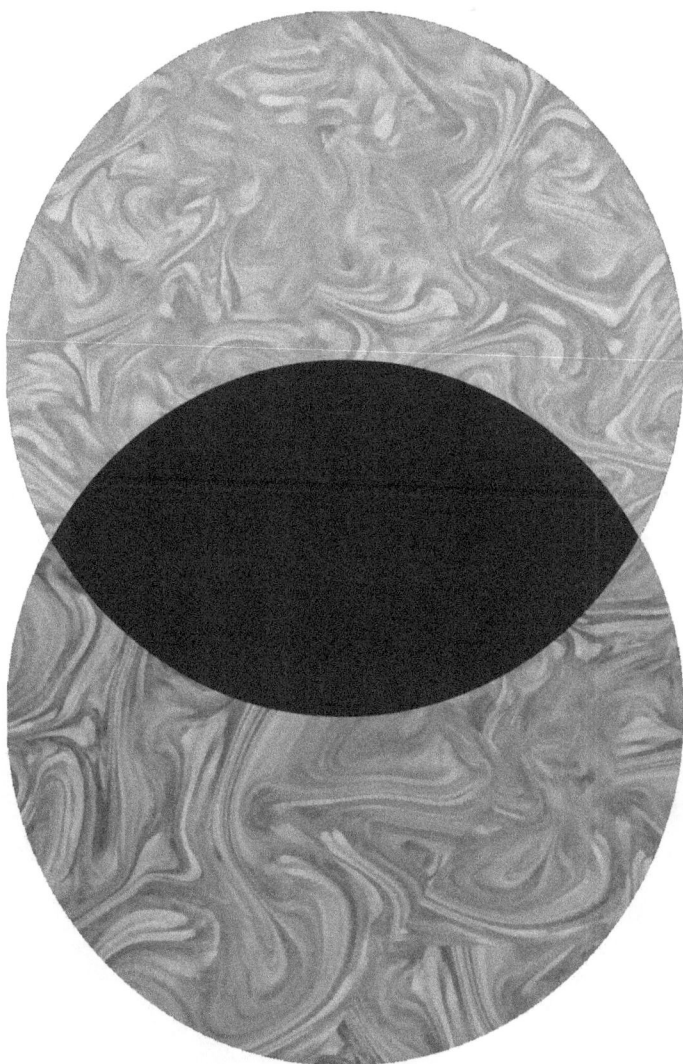

CHAPTER 9

"Hence I remind you to rekindle the gift of God that is within you through the laying on of my hands; for God did not give us a spirit of timidity but a spirit of power and love and self-control."

The Second Letter of Paul
to Timothy 1: 6 and 7

Control of the self requires discipline. Discipline is training that is expected to produce a specific character or pattern of behavior, especially training that produces moral or mental improvement.

A law professor once taught me that analysis means "to break down into component parts." We must begin analyzing the self in order to control the self. In other words, we must break down the self into its component parts. The parts of the self are: the physical self including the senses, the mental, intellectual, and knowing self, the sleeping or subconscious self including Jungian archetypal symbols, the emotional and emotive self of feelings and passions, and the contemplative or mystical self of union with The Ultimate Reality, God.

The physical self is your body and your senses. This is the most dangerous and most corruptible part of your being. Your body and its senses are the Devil's amusement park. "[T]he spirit indeed is willing, but the flesh is weak." (See *Matthew 26: 41*). You should know by now what your physical weaknesses are. What tempts you? What impulses, fantasies, or compulsive behaviors rule you? This is not only the realm of sexual weaknesses but also overeating, oversleeping, and excessive drinking. You can also be guilty of neglecting yourself for the sake of others: children, spouses, friends, employers, customers, or parents. The worst caregivers are those who forget to first care for themselves. Exercise and nutrition are helpful tools. Make them your friends. Rule your body with self-control. Your mood, soul, and mind will reward you.

The knowing self is also susceptible, because of its tendency to puffing and pride, the vitamins of arrogance. The fall of Lucifer is the story of his rebellion against the divine. Satan's arrogance and pride are his weaknesses. Let us recall The King of Babylon (See *Isaiah 14*). This reference to an earthly king is actually the story of Satan's fall from the kingdom of God in addition to a story of a king.

Chapter 9

Isaiah writes:

> "How you are fallen from heaven,
>> O Day Star, son of Dawn!
> How you are cut down to the ground,
>> you who laid the nations low!
> You said in your heart,
>> 'I will set my throne on high;
> I will sit on the mount of assembly
>> in the far north;
> I will ascend above the heights of the
>> Clouds,
> I will make myself like the Most
>> High.'
> But you are brought down to Sheol,
>> to the depths of the Pit."

(See *Isaiah 14: 12–15*)

The knowing self is easily tempted into pride, self-centeredness, and rebellion against God, The Author of Life. "...So do not become proud, but stand in awe..." (See *Romans 11: 20*).

The third self, the subconscious or sleeping self, is both fascinating and difficult to understand. Complex symbols, archetypes, ambiguities, and double meanings confuse the language of the subconscious. You have a subconscious or unconscious self that centers, disturbs, balances, pushes, and throws your other selves. It is beyond your control. It is a strange, productive, and murky apparatus of humanity. Study this subject, write down your night dreams, read Jung, and learn to interpret the multiple meanings of your dreams and the blurred workings of your subconscious. This part of your self is difficult but it can be mastered.

Fourth, you feel to be yourself. You laugh, cry, shout, and love. You experience a spectrum of emotions and passions. Have your feelings ever been hurt? What was the saddest moment of your life? Your feeling or emotional self is complicated, biochemical, and ethereal. Sometimes the particular emotion you experience is not as important as your reaction to it. It is not your emotions that arise which matter so much as your choices and reactions to those feelings. You have a choice. You have power, love, and self-control.

Fifth, we find your contemplative self by looking for the sun inside closed eyes. Not prayer—by which we talk to God. But rather, meditation or contemplation by which God seeks to unite with us.

"Do you not know that your body is a temple of the Holy Spirit within you, which you have from God? You are not your own; you were bought with a price. So glorify God in your body." (See *1 Corinthians 6: 19 and 20*).

Did you hear that? Your body is a temple! Not your temple, but God's temple and the Holy Spirit's temple. This is part of the mystery of spiritual life. God does not go exclusively to a church, synagogue, or cathedral to join you. He goes to your body, His temple! When God or the Holy Spirit arrives at this temple, are your front doors open? Mystical union with The Eternal One occurs inside of you. You are God's temple!

But it is not that easy. Jesus himself was tempted in the wilderness. Matthew tells us, in Chapter 4, Verses 1 through 11, of three specific weapons the Devil uses for corruption. Thankfully, Matthew also instructs us how to defend ourselves from these weapons of personal destruction. Heed you the word:

> Then Jesus was led up by the Spirit into the wilderness to be tempted by the devil. And he fasted forty days and forty nights, and afterward he was hungry. And the tempter came and said to him, "If you are the Son of God, command these stones to become loaves of bread." But he answered, "It is written, 'Man shall not live by bread alone, but by every word that proceeds from the mouth of God.'" Then the devil took him to the holy city, and set him on the pinnacle of the temple, and said to him, "If you are the Son of God, throw yourself down; for it is written, 'He will give his angels charge

of you,' and 'On their hands they will bear you up, lest you strike your foot against a stone.'" Jesus said to him, "Again it is written, 'You shall not tempt the Lord your God.'" Again, the devil took him to a very high mountain, and showed him all the kingdoms of the world and the glory of them; and he said to him, "All these I will give you, if you will fall down and worship me." Then Jesus said to him, "Begone, Satan! for it is written, 'You shall worship the Lord your God and him only shall you serve.'" Then the devil left him, and behold, angels came and ministered to him.

(See *Matthew 4: 1–11*).

This passage is fascinating. Note that it was the Spirit (and not Satan) that led Jesus to be tempted. God will tempt you and allow you to be tempted by others in your life. This is for your own good "...that he might humble you and test you, to do you good in the end." (See *Deuteronomy 8: 16*).

Three weapons of Satan are challenge and hunger/desire, challenge and tempting God, and seduction of power and glory in exchange for worship and rebellion against the Lord.

God will allow Satan to test and to tempt you throughout your life to challenge your faith and your heart. Read the book of Job sometime for further proof of this. Evil will try to use your hungers and physical desires to turn you. Evil will try anything to get you to tempt God and go against His Word. Evil tries to seduce us with worldly power and glory in exchange for our rebellion against the Lord.

Will you choose the bread of The Tempter over The Word of your Lord when you are hungry? Will you choose to tempt God when you are challenged? Will you choose the earthly things (wealth, power, sex, fame) over God's will for your life?

The tester challenges us with statements like "If you are _____, then do _____." You do not have to prove yourself to Darkness. You only have to prove yourself to the Light.

Jesus responds to each of the three tests with "It is written..." Jesus expresses God's will through quotation from The Holy Scriptures, not by choosing or using his own words. What a great shield from the weapons of deceit! This is the toughest armor. The Word is your shield, your armor, and the strength of your defense. You have a fortress wall of protection around you when you invoke God's will through the expression of scripture in times of testing, tormenting, and tempting. Remember to say in times of your greatest crises, "It is written..." You have spiritual weapons at your disposal.

But, be careful and precise with scripture, because we see how the Devil also quotes (or misquotes) scripture. Do not twist or pervert the words of The Holy Bible. Know the scriptures. Know them well.

Finally, please remember that even the only Son of God needed angels to come and to minister to him after his temptations. How much more do you, a son or daughter of man, need angels to minister to you! It is okay to let other people help you in your times of need.

Control of the self requires discipline. Discipline is training that is expected to produce a specific character or pattern of behavior, especially training that produces moral or mental improvement. Apply discipline to all of your selves: physical, mental, subconscious, emotional, and contemplative. Defend yourself. Defend your God. Draw out your most powerful sword of all, "It is written..."

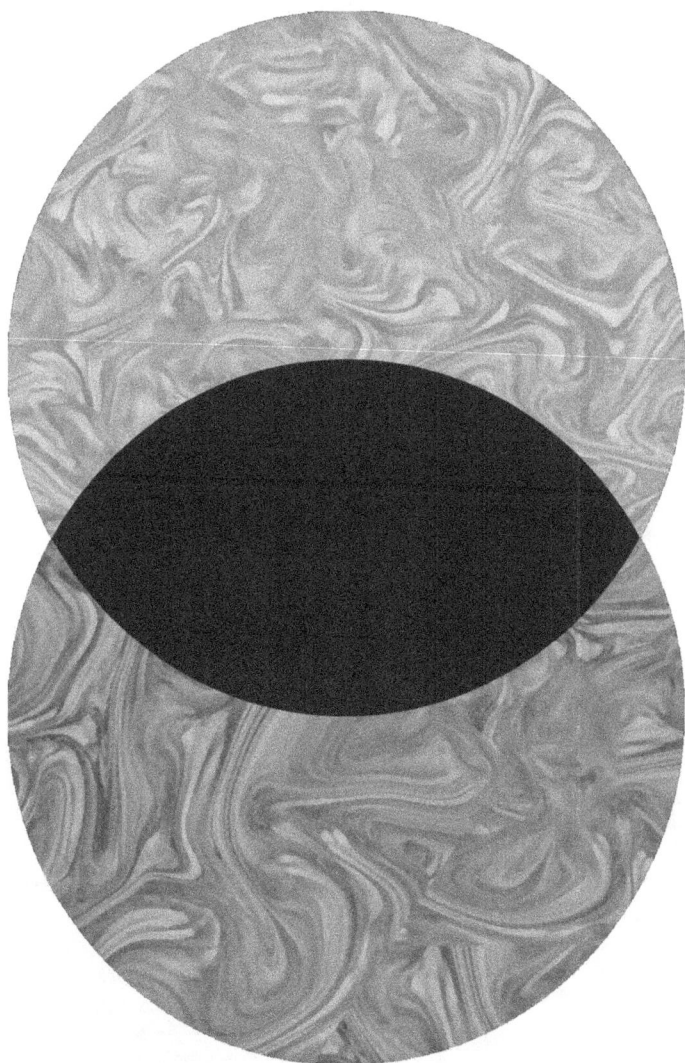

CHAPTER 10

"...[F]or God did not give us a spirit of timidity..." God gave us a spirit of power, love, and self-control, the gift of God. May we think for a moment about what God did not give us?

Timidity is the state of shrinking from dangerous or difficult circumstances. It is hesitancy or fearfulness. The word derives from the Latin word *timere*, meaning to fear. This is *not* the spirit God gave us. God did *not* give us a spirit of shrinking, hesitancy, and fearfulness. He gave us a spirit of power, love, and self-control.

What do you fear the most? Being alone? Unhappiness? Poverty? Having your sins discovered? Disease? Dying? The loss of a relationship? Divorce? Jail? Alienation from your parents? Your children? Unemployment?

Fear is a playground of the Devil and his demons. You are not being true to yourself when you give in to fear. Didn't God give you a spirit of power, love, and self- control?

You must first recognize your fears to master them. You will cheat yourself of being who you really are until you realize that you are thinking, acting, and behaving out of fear. You have power. You have love. You have self-control. Why do you think Jesus told Satan "Begone, Satan"? Jesus was saying to Satan (and to fear, temptation, testing, and tormenting) that Jesus did not have a spirit of timidity, but of power, love, and self-control.

"Begone, fear," is a good way to train your mind when you experience doubt, hesitancy, or shrinking from dangerous or difficult circumstances. Notice again that we are discussing another variation on the theme that the Way is not easy, but hard. The Lord does not tell us that we will not face dangerous or difficult circumstances. Rather, we *will* face dangerous or difficult circumstances: count on it. We must rely upon our power, love, and self-control when we face tough situations.

Birds discovered the live oak one year. At first the zenzontles (mockingbirds) would alight upon its branches, if only for a moment. They darted in, took cover, and did their scouting. The mockingbirds moved on.

Later, songbirds gravitated to the former shoot. They lingered, flitted, and tended to themselves. And then the songbirds sang. Oh, how they sang! If only angels could sing as well as the songbirds that blessed our yard.

Chapter 10

The live oak became more than a young tree. It was now a shelter. It was now a safe place for music, for nature's symphony. It still was curved, but the songbirds did not see that part of the tree beneath their perches.

Music amplified across the yard from the live oak. Music came from the thing I almost cut down with a lawnmower years before. What other things did I cut down in my life? Who did I stop from growing when I should have chosen life and fighting chances? Who did I forget to tend to? Who did I neglect to love?

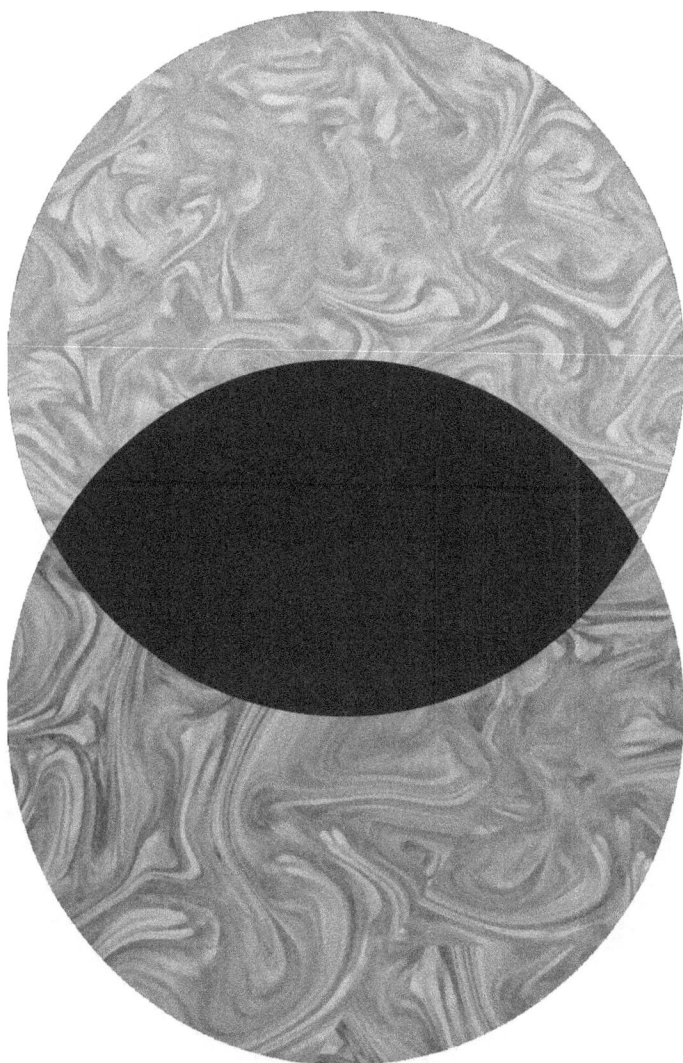

CHAPTER 11

Self-control applies to all aspects of our lives including our moments of Christian meditation. We looked, in the previous two chapters, at trials and tests as well as fearful thinking as appropriate times to exercise self-control. Our power, our love, and our self-control are utilized in the social world, but we must use them in our inner lives too.

Warning. Do not look for yourself when you close your eyes to meditate. Do not look for yourself when you close your eyes to open your heart, mind, soul, and strength to the Ancient of Days.

It is easy to nap.

It is easy to fantasize.

It is easy to think about work and things to do.

It is easy to think about your problems.

It is easy to think about people and relationships.

It is easy to think about money.

It is easy to think about yourself.

You are not inviting the Creator to communion if you are thinking about yourself during contemplative moments. That is why it is important to say the divine names. It is imperative to focus on God. There is a space left and it is open for God when your ego, thoughts, and self-preoccupations slip away.

The steep climb up The Mount of Contemplation is crowded with distractions and diversions. This is a way of wrong turns. It is easy to step off the path and fall down the Cliff of Self. To rise, and to reach the summit, your climbing ability is inversely correlated with your ability to let your cares, thoughts, and impulses drift away.

It is easy, but wrong, to pray while you meditate. We all have our petitions, but the contemplative life is not the life of requests, prayers, and wishes. The contemplative life is a search for darkness, for the cloud of unknowing, for the loss of self and selfishness, and for the seeking without wanting. You are building a spiritual room within your soul where The Divine may visit on your invitation. "In my Father's house are many rooms..." (See *John 14:2*).

These metaphysical subjects do not make sense. Uniting with God is not about intellectual attainment. Knowledge has no legs in this place of the soul. You cannot "know" God anyway, because God's face is hidden on earth. "No one has ever seen God..." (See *John 1: 18*).

Solomon did not ask God for knowledge, but for wisdom and understanding. Solomon's father, David, played the lyre and danced naked, to the disgust of his first wife, Michal. David sang and wrote poetry. He also was a bloody butcher in battle. Nonetheless, David regularly went into a cave to find his strength in the Lord.

Sometimes we go into a cave to elude our enemies. Other times, we go into a cave to be still. This was the "wilderness" for Jesus. Jesus was angry at Simon Peter when he fell asleep at night when he should have been praying or meditating. Do not fall asleep when your eyes are closed and The Lord is near.

There is darkness when you close your eyes. There is light when you close your eyes. Do you not see that it is all the same? He who made the light also made the darkness. He made you, too.

The darkness, the wilderness, the stillness, the cave, the chair in a quiet room in your house, the garden, dancing naked, and the cloud of unknowing are all the same. They are the place, time, and will to lose yourself so you may be touched by the Light. Close your eyes to be transformed by the Light of Eternity and the Eternity of Light.

Moses, for example, was changed forever when he returned to the base of Mount Sinai. The presence of God will do that. Moses went alone. He climbed, struggled, bowed, stayed, and returned. After the union with God, Moses was transformed, his face different.

The sun inside closed eyes is like the sun in the sky. It is life-giving, life-affirming, and life-altering. There are times when it is gone. Those times are called night. However, the moon itself reminds us that the light is not gone, but simply in its cycle. Isn't it remarkable that the speed of light is one place where time can slow down or stop? 186,000 miles per second can stop or slow down time. We do not really understand light completely, but we can look for it—especially with our eyes closed.

I try to imagine the Transfiguration of Jesus. (See *Mark 9: 1-8*). What did it look like? It was as white as white can be and as bright as bright can be. Is that all? Moses was there. Elijah was there. What did they look like after centuries? How peculiar and startling it must have been for Peter, James, and John to witness.

Search The Holy Bible for physical descriptions of God. It is a daunting task. When I say "Jesus," what image comes to your mind's eye? Long hair? Western European or American? White? Tall? Thin? Kindly face? Asian? Bearded?

The paintings and portraits of Jesus over the ages are not accurate. Jesus was Jewish. His mother was Jewish. He was born in Bethlehem and raised in Nazareth. He was Galilean. But we do not know if he was tall or short, brown or black eyed, bearded or shaven, soft or rough, skinny or fat. Joseph was not Jesus' biological father. The genetics become fuzzy when a divine child is conceived by a human mother and God's will.

My guess is that there are no good descriptions of Jesus' physical traits for a reason: the Lord of The Old Testament kept (and keeps) his face hidden. We are to seek Him out nevertheless. David writes, in Psalm 27: 8 and 9, "Thou hast said, 'Seek ye my face.' My heart says to thee, 'Thy face, Lord, do I seek.' Hide not thy face from me.'"

Does anyone find it noteworthy that of all the stories, tales, parables, and testimonies of Jesus, none paint a portrait of what he looked like? Is not this the same God, Old Testament and New, who keeps his face hidden in the earth forever?

Remember these words:

"...and his face was like the sun shining in full strength."

The Revelation to John 1: 16.

Can you look directly at the sun shining in full strength? No. You blind yourself if you do. The Lord, also, is too bright for our earthly eyes. We have to look away or down.

We have to close our eyes. The Lord is too much for us. The Lord is pure light in full strength.

It must be that we are not meant to see God's face on earth. It must be that we are not meant to see his face as one of ours. The sun inside closed eyes cannot be photographed, videotaped, recorded, or painted. The film is overexposed when the sun is shining in full strength. Close your eyes and you will see. You will see without your eyes.

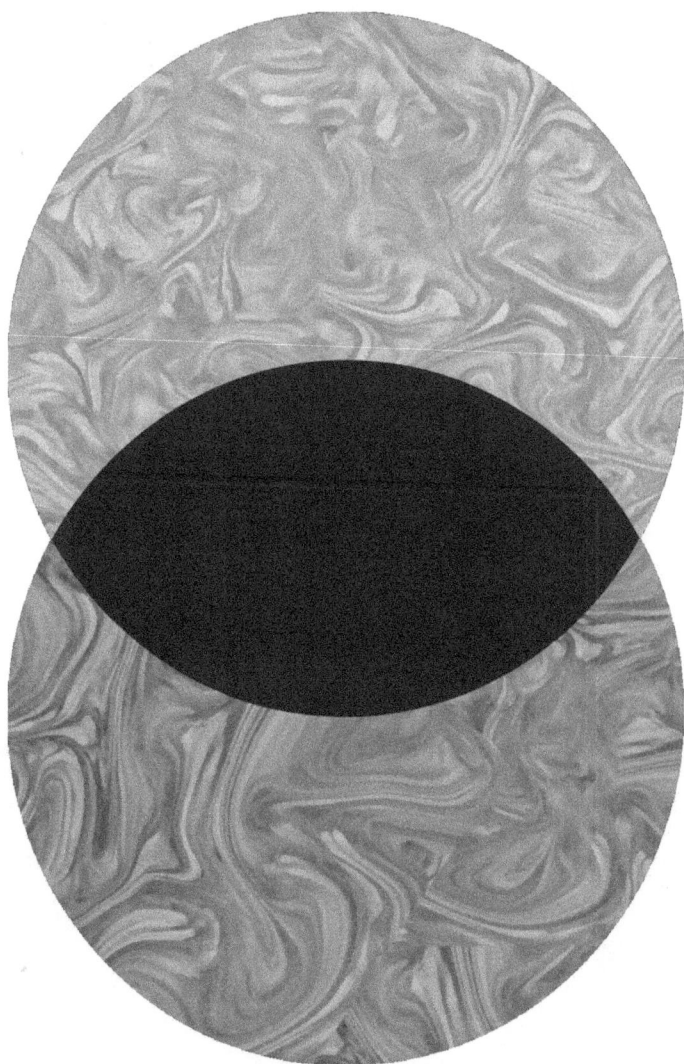

CHAPTER 12

Our little shoot in the backyard is now a tall live oak. We cut down the cedar tree to make room for a wood deck. Its stump is covered in darkness and it will not grow again. The cedar is dead.

The yucca is still there. It flowers madly each year. It is sharp, dangerous, and pretty. It is not as tall as the shoot that became a tree.

The live oak did a miraculous thing. It straightened itself out. Its lower half is still curved outward as a memorial to its fighting youth. But it grew a little backward from its curve to grow straight and tall above its curve. It is now fifteen years old and counting. It provides shade to the house and the grass. It protects and guards the home when the hard rains and bullying winds come.

The tiny sprout, that I let live, is now a focal point in the yard. It is one of the first things you notice when you stand on the deck. Its leaves are a comforting shade of green. For South Texas, it is a gift from the heat. For South Texas, it is a survivor. It fought against the cedar for water for years. It won with persistence.

The Sun Inside Closed Eyes

The skinny shoot that became a live oak shares the sunshine with the moody yucca. They coexist. The live oak thrives, survives, and displays its curvature. It reminds all that see it, that it was tested, tormented, and even twisted for a time.

Then, though, the shoot became what it was meant to be, by stretching and reaching daily for the light. Each and every minute it contended with the shadows in its space. It fought so it could grow. The sunshine triumphed. The sunshine grew what I first thought was a weed into a solid, shade-giving tree. That tree is pleasing and attractive in a graceful and delicate way.

You are like the live oak. You can stretch and reach for the light, the sun inside closed eyes.

BIBLIOGRAPHY

_____, *The Cloud of Unknowing.* New York: Penguin Classics, 1978.

Epstein, Perle. *Kabbalah: The Way of the Jewish Mystic.* Boston: Shambhala Classics, 1978.

Finley, James. *Christian Meditation: Experiencing the Presence of God.* San Francisco: HarperCollins, 2004.

God. *The Holy Bible.* Multiple Publishers, Outside of Time and Space.

Merton, Thomas. *Choosing to Love the World.* Canada: Sounds True, 2008.

Missler, Chuck. *Cosmic Codes: Hidden Messages from the Edge of Eternity.* Couer d'Alene, Idaho: Koinonia House, 1999.

Schroeder, Gerald L. *The Hidden Face of God: Science Reveals the Ultimate Truth.* New York: Simon & Schuster, 2001.

BIBLE VERSES
CITED IN ORDER

The Revelation to John 1: 16

The Second Letter of Paul to Timothy 1: 6 and 7

Philippians 4: 11-13

Luke 17: 20-21

Leviticus 17: 11 and 14

Romans 12: 11

Mark 12: 28-34

Isaiah 6: 10

Philippians 2: 13

1 Corinthians 13

Hebrews 13: 1 and 2

Matthew 26: 41

Isaiah 14

Romans 11: 20

1 Corinthians 6: 19 and 20

Matthew 4: 1-11

Deuteronomy 8: 16

John 14: 2

John 1: 18

Mark 9: 1-8

Psalm 27: 8 and 9

MEDITATION

BREATHE IN	BREATHE OUT

Breathe In	Breathe Out
Breathe In	Breathe Out
Breathe In	Breathe Out

God loves me	I love God
God loves me	I love God
God loves me	I love God

I am present, open,	and awake
I am present, open,	and awake
I am present, open,	and awake

Here I am,	Lord
Here I am,	Lord
Here I am,	Lord

Be still	and know that I am the Lord
Be still	and know that I am the Lord
Be still	and know that I am the Lord

Be still	and know
Be still	and know
Be still	and know

The Sun Inside Closed Eyes

BREATHE IN	BREATHE OUT
Be	still
Be	still
Be	still
Be	
Be	
Be	
Adonai	Sovereignty and My Lord
Adonai	Sovereignty and My Lord
Adonai	Sovereignty and My Lord
El Shaddai	Foundation
El Shaddai	Foundation
El Shaddai	Foundation
Elohim	Judgment
Elohim	Judgment
Elohim	Judgment
Yahweh	Wisdom and Understanding
Yahweh	Wisdom and Understanding
Yahweh	Wisdom and Understanding

BREATHE IN	BREATHE OUT
Ehyeh	Crown of Humility
Ehyeh	Crown of Humility
Ehyeh	Crown of Humility
Jesus	God with us
Jesus	God with us
Jesus	God with us
Holy Spirit	In-dwelling
Holy Spirit	In-dwelling
Holy Spirit	In-dwelling
Father, Son,	and Holy Ghost
Father, Son,	and Holy Ghost
Father, Son,	and Holy Ghost
Holy	Trinity
Holy	Trinity
Holy	Trinity
Power, Love, and	Self-Control
Power, Love, and	Self-Control
Power, Love, and	Self-Control

The Sun Inside Closed Eyes

BREATHE IN	BREATHE OUT
I can do all things in Him	who strengthens me
I can do all things in Him	who strengthens me
I can do all things in Him	who strengthens me
God loves me	I love God
God loves me	I love God
God loves me	I love God
Breathe In	Breathe Out
Breathe In	Breathe Out
Breathe In	Breathe Out.

NOTES

The Sun Inside Closed Eyes

Notes

The Sun Inside Closed Eyes

Notes

Notes

Notes

Notes

Notes

Notes

ABOUT THE AUTHOR

Stephen L. Avard, Jr. received a Bachelor of Arts degree with majors in history, political science, and legal studies from Rice University in 1987 and a Juris Doctorate from The Texas Tech University School of Law in 1992. For sixteen years, he practiced commercial litigation law across the State of Texas, primarily in San Antonio, and today he is a successful real estate investor and President of Maidstone Real Estate, Inc. A Christian for almost four decades, Avard has studied The Holy Bible for many years, believes anyone can achieve enlightenment through Christian meditation, and teaches that Christian mysticism is an overlooked tool of faith that can change lives. An independent publisher of transformative books, he recently founded Avard Enterprises, LLC. Author of *The Sun Inside Closed Eyes*, Avard is a family man and a servant of God who writes and lives in Houston, Texas and Mount Crested Butte, Colorado.

To learn more and to contact the author please visit *www.SteveAvard.com*.

www.ingramcontent.com/pod-product-compliance
Lightning Source LLC
Chambersburg PA
CBHW061745020426
42331CB00006B/1363